SUPER SANDCASTLE™

Animal Habitats

What Lives in the Desert?

Oona Gaarder-Juntti

Consulting Editor, Diane Craig, M.A./Reading Specialist

ABDO Publishing Company

Published by ABDO Publishing Company, 8000 West 78th Street, Edina, Minnesota 55439. Copyright © 2009 by Abdo Consulting Group, Inc. International copyrights reserved in all countries. No part of this book may be reproduced in any form without written permission from the publisher. Super SandCastle™ is a trademark and logo of ABDO Publishing Company.

Printed in the United States.

Credits
Editor: Liz Salzmann
Content Developer: Nancy Tuminelly
Cover and Interior Design and Production: Oona Gaarder-Juntti, Mighty Media
Illustration: Oona Gaarder-Juntti
Photo Credits: iStockphoto/Alan Hewitt, iStockphoto/JohnBillingslea, ShutterStock, Stockdisc

Library of Congress Cataloging-in-Publication Data

Gaarder-Juntti, Oona, 1979-

  What lives in the desert? / Oona Gaarder-Juntti.

    p. cm. -- (Animal habitats)

  ISBN 978-1-60453-173-2

  1. Desert animals--Juvenile literature. 2. Desert ecology--Juvenile literature. I. Title.

  QL116.G33 2008

  591.754--dc22

                          2008005477

Super SandCastle™ books are created by a team of professional educators, reading specialists, and content developers around five essential components— phonemic awareness, phonics, vocabulary, text comprehension, and fluency— to assist young readers as they develop reading skills and strategies and increase their general knowledge. All books are written, reviewed, and leveled for guided reading, early reading intervention, and Accelerated Reader® programs for use in shared, guided, and independent reading and writing activities to support a balanced approach to literacy instruction.

About SUPER SANDCASTLE™

Bigger Books for Emerging Readers
Grades K–4

Created for library, classroom, and at-home use, Super SandCastle™ books support and engage young readers as they develop and build literacy skills and will increase their general knowledge about the world around them. Super SandCastle™ books are part of SandCastle™, the leading PreK–3 imprint for emerging and beginning readers. Super SandCastle™ features a larger trim size for more reading fun.

Let Us Know
Super SandCastle™ would like to hear your stories about reading this book. What was your favorite page? Was there something hard that you needed help with? Share the ups and downs of learning to read. We want to hear from you! Send us an e-mail.

sandcastle@abdopublishing.com

Contact us for a complete list of SandCastle™, Super SandCastle™, and other nonfiction and fiction titles from ABDO Publishing Company.

www.abdopublishing.com • 8000 West 78th Street Edina, MN 55439 • 800-800-1312 • 952-831-1632 fax

One-fifth of the earth's surface is desert. Deserts get less than 10 inches of rain per year so they are very dry. There are hot deserts and cold deserts.

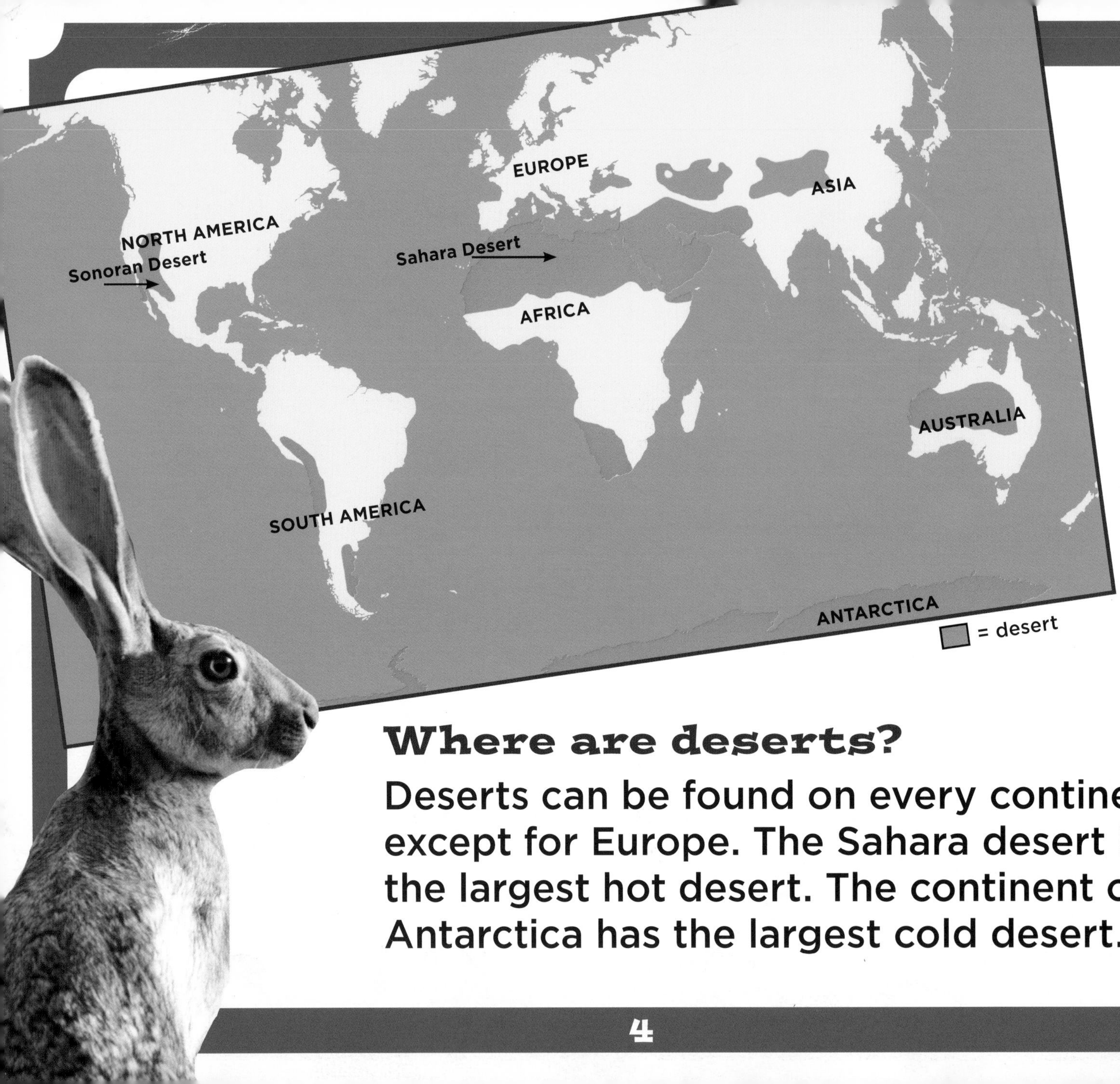
EUROPE
ASIA
NORTH AMERICA
Sonoran Desert
Sahara Desert
AFRICA
AUSTRALIA
SOUTH AMERICA
ANTARCTICA
= desert

Where are deserts?

Deserts can be found on every continent except for Europe. The Sahara desert is the largest hot desert. The continent of Antarctica has the largest cold desert.

What does the desert look like?

Every desert has different plants and animals that have adapted to living there. The plants and animals in the Sonoran Desert include cactuses, roadrunners, and reptiles.

GILA MONSTER

Animal class: Reptile
Location: North America

Gila monsters can be up to two feet long. They are the largest lizards in the United States. Gila monsters are poisonous. There is only one other poisonous lizard in the world.

Gila monsters often go for months without eating. They can live off the fat stored in their tails.

FENNEC FOX

Animal class: Mammal
Location: Africa

Fennec foxes are the smallest of all foxes. They have unusually large ears for their size. Their large ears help them stay cool by giving off body heat.

Fennec foxes spend the day in their burrows. They hunt for food at night when it's cooler.

WESTERN DIAMONDBACK RATTLESNAKE

Animal class: Reptile
Location: North America

The western diamondback rattlesnake is one of the most dangerous rattlesnakes in North America. A new section is added to the rattle on its tail each time the snake sheds its skin.

Diamondback rattlesnakes use their tongues to smell their surroundings.

ECHIDNA

Animal class: Mammal
Location: Australia

Echidnas are mammals but they lay eggs. They use their claws to open up ant nests. Echidnas use their sticky tongues to quickly catch and eat the ants.

The echidna has a long nose with a tiny mouth. It can open its mouth just enough to stick out its tongue.

MEERKAT

Animal class: Mammal
Location: Africa

Meerkats live together in large groups called mobs. Meerkats stand up on their back legs to watch for predators. They call out to the others if there is danger.

Meerkats spend their days looking for food, grooming, playing, and sunbathing.

LAPPET-FACED VULTURE

Animal class: Bird
Location: Africa

The lappet-faced vulture is the largest vulture in Africa. It has a strong beak that it uses to tear apart its food. Its head and face are bald so it can easily clean itself after eating.

The lappet-faced vulture has a wingspan of eight to nine feet.

ORYX

Animal class: Mammal
Location: Africa

Oryx are a type of antelope. They travel across the desert in large herds. Oryx can go for a long time without drinking water. Both male and female oryx have long, thin horns.

Male oryx will use their horns to fight over a female or territory.

18

BACTRIAN CAMEL

Animal class: Mammal
Location: Asia

Bactrian camels have two humps. They live in the cold Gobi desert. Their humps are used to store fat. They can go for long periods of time without food or water.

Camels turn the fat in their humps into energy. As the fat is used, their humps become floppy.

Have you ever been to a desert?

More Desert Animals

Can you learn about these desert animals?

armadillo	jack rabbit
bandicoot	jeroboa
caracal	long-nosed bat
desert locust	ostrich
desert tortoise	puma
dingo	roadrunner
dung beetle	scorpion
elf owl	sidewinder viper
hyena	thorny devil

GLOSSARY

adapt – to change in order to function better for a specific need or situation.

burrow – a hole or tunnel dug in the ground by a small animal for use as shelter.

cactus – a plant with sharp spikes instead of leaves that grows in hot dry places.

continent – one of seven large land masses on earth. The continents are Asia, Africa, Europe, North America, South America, Australia, and Antarctica.

dangerous – able or likely to cause harm or injury.

energy – the ability to move, work, or play hard without getting tired.

groom – to clean the fur of an animal.

mammal – a warm-blooded animal that has hair and whose females produce milk to feed the young.

predator – an animal that hunts others.

shed – to lose something, such as skin, leaves, or fur, through a natural process.

wingspan – the distance from one wing tip to the other when the wings are fully spread.